Introduction

"The earnest (heartfelt, continued) prayer of a righteous man makes tremendous power available [dynamic in its working]."

James 5:16 AMP

Prayer is fellowshipping with the Father – a vital, personal contact with God Who is more than enough and wants to meet your daily needs.

Prayer is not to be a meaningless religious ritual with no power. It is to be effective and accurate and bring *results*.

God watches over His Word to perform it. (Jer. 1:12.) That is why we designed this special edition of *Prayers That Avail Much* – to give you the opportunity to pray God's Word and watch Him fulfill His promises.

Based upon the bestselling original book, *Prayers That Avail Much, Volume 2*, this compact, easy-to-use edition offers a scriptural prayer and a faith-filled confession to help you speak the Word. As you pray these scriptural prayers, your faith will grow and your heart will be encouraged.

Prayers That Avail Much, Volume 2, Portable Gift Book – praying with the power of God's Word!

Prayers That Avail Much

Volume 2

The Effectual Fervent Prayer
Of a Righteous Man Availeth Much

Harrison House, Inc
Tulsa, Oklahoma

Prayers That Avail Much, Volume 2, Portable Gift Book
ISBN 0-89274-963-6
Copyright © 1995 by
Harrison House, Inc.
P. O. Box 35035
Tulsa, OK 74153

Published by HARRISON HOUSE, INC.
P. O. Box 35035
Tulsa, OK 74153

Father God, thank You for teaching me the principles of giving. You will never be outdone with the giving of any man or woman. Instead, You return to me, and every other person, in proportion to that which we give. Because I sow bountifully, I receive bountifully. This financial principle applies to other areas of life. Bountiful giving, bountiful receiving. Stingy giving, meager receiving. I am a bountiful, generous, cheerful and prompt to do it giver, in Jesus' name. My harvest is continual and abundant. Hallelujah!

2 Corinthians 9:6-12

———————————— CONFESSION ————————————

I live to give rather than give to live!

Heavenly Father, You said through Paul that I am an epistle that reveals Jesus Christ, known and read of all men. Help me, Lord, because I want Your epistle (Your Word) in me and in my lifestyle to represent You accurately. You said this epistle is not written down in ink, but it is written by Your Spirit. It is not written in tables of stone, but in the fleshly table of my heart. In the name of Jesus, I will represent You well, Father God. Amen.

2 Corinthians 3:1-3

—————— CONFESSION ——————

My heart contains the epistles of Jesus Christ,
and my tongue is as the pen of a ready writer! (Ps. 45:1.)

Heavenly Father, I accept Samuel's admonishment to the Israelites. It is as fresh and accurate today as when he spoke it, because it was Holy Spirit inspired. I will serve You with all my heart. Father, in Jesus' name. I have turned from wickedness, and it shall never be a part of me again. Thank You for Your promise that You will never forsake me, because You have called me Yours! In You, I am accepted and I belong! You have done great things for me, Lord! Hallelujah!

1 Samuel 12:20-25

──────────────── CONFESSION ────────────────

God's ways are perfect. I will follow His example and walk in the good and the right way!

Father, Joshua and Caleb had what was referred to as "another spirit." This means they had an excellent or a superior spirit – one that was distinctive, premium, outstanding, of highest or supreme rank. You implied that a person with this kind of spirit followed you "fully." Help me to follow You fully in the name of Jesus and to be known as a person who has a first-class spirit! Amen.

Numbers 14:24

---— CONFESSION ———

I have an excellent spirit, which causes me
to do courageous feats for God's Kingdom!

Father God, You said that one can put a thousand to flight and two can put ten thousand to flight. I join forces with believers of like faith to put the devil on the run. He flees from me as in great terror and horror! I will take my place in the Body of Christ. I will not be forgetful to assemble myself together with the Body on a consistent basis. In Jesus' name, a unified Body will make mighty power available to defeat the enemy. Hallelujah!

Deuteronomy 32:30; Hebrews 10:25

CONFESSION

I will be alert for opportunities to edify, exhort, comfort and come into agreement with other believers to cause God's Kingdom to increase in mighty power upon the earth.

Father God, in Jesus' name, help me to keep my focus on You, for You said if my mind is fixed on You, You will keep me in perfect peace. You also said that the work of righteousness would produce peace in my heart and life. Thank You for giving me Your righteousness when I was born again, Lord Jesus, in exchange for my own righteousness, which was as filthy rags. I bind the messenger of Satan who has been loosed to bring chaos to my dwelling place, and I loose and accept the peaceable habitation You promised me, Father God, in Jesus' name. Amen.

Isaiah 26:3; Isaiah 32:17,18; Isaiah 64:6

———————— C O N F E S S I O N ————————

God, also known as Jehovah Shalom, is peace to me!

Father, although Mary didn't fully understand how she would conceive Your Son, Jesus Christ, because she had not known a man intimately, she believed the word of the angel. Her response was, "Be it unto me according to thy word." Father, thank You for the destiny to which You have called me. Like Mary, I believe You, that there will be a performance of those things – all of them – which You have spoken to my heart personally and through Your Word, in the name of Jesus. Amen.

Luke 1:28-45

——————————— C O N F E S S I O N ———————————

I will magnify the Lord, because nothing,
absolutely nothing, is impossible with Him!

 Heavenly Father, You gave Your Son, Jesus Christ, to redeem me from all iniquity and to purify me as a peculiar or special person. You have ordained me to be zealous or fervent for good works. Help me to bring honor to You today, Lord, with the work of my hands. Thank You for causing Holy Ghost advertising and connections to promote every work that enhances and advances Your Kingdom, in Jesus' name. Amen.

Titus 2:14

———————— C O N F E S S I O N ————————

The Holy Spirit is orchestrating advertising, connections and promotions for the work I am doing for God's Kingdom.

Father, in Jesus' name, You are never slack in the performance of Your promises. You respond quickly to the person who operates in faith, believing and speaking Your Word and accepting it at face value. My trust is in You and Your Word, Father. Your Word is the source of all truth in my life. I have set my face as a flint that as I believe and speak Your Word, I have its promises! It is mine, and I'll not be denied. Hallelujah!

Isaiah 50:7; 2 Peter 3:9

———————— CONFESSION ————————

Because I trust in God's Word, I will never be brought to shame. Your Word sets me apart from the norm as a reputable leader!

Father, thank You for helping me to enlarge the place of my tent and to strengthen my stakes. This is the hour to reach out to others in every way possible with the Good News of You, Lord Jesus! In You there is hope for despair. In You there is stability for upheaval. In You there is prosperity for lack. In You there is health and healing for sickness and disease. In You there is peace for war, whether it is in a relationship, in the home, or in my land. In You, Lord Jesus, is well-being for every area of life! Hallelujah!

Isaiah 54:2,3

———————————— C O N F E S S I O N ————————————

The Holy Spirit divinely orchestrates every aspect of my life!

Father, You have emphasized the importance of walking in unity and harmony. My house will stand, for we are not divided. My work and ministry assignments will be effective because there is oneness and harmony in place of strife. Your Kingdom in this earth is growing in power and might, Father, because we are learning how to walk in love and cover one another's differences in prayer. We are learning to be selfless rather than selfish, in Jesus' name. Hallelujah!

Matthew 12:25

———————————— CONFESSION ————————————

I will walk in perfect unity
with my brothers and sisters in Christ!

Father, it is Your desire to do signs, wonders and miracles in our midst, particularly to draw unbelievers into Your Kingdom – to cause them to become believers! You also provide miracles to bless Your people, Lord, and cause them to be blessed above anything the world has to offer! To set the stage for miracles, You have asked that I be sanctified. Holy Spirit, You are the only One Who can sanctify me wholly. I yield to Your cleansing and construction work, in Jesus' name. Amen.

Joshua 3:5

C O N F E S S I O N

I am being reconstructed in the Carpenter's Shop
to be exactly what God wants me to be!

Father, in the name of Jesus, awaken me if I have been sluggish, lazy, complacent or negligent to hear and then obey the Holy Spirit. I will arise from dullness to Your Spirit. Flood me with the light of Your Word, Lord. To walk in Your "highest kind of life, love and light" Father, takes the leading of Your Spirit. Help me to be more spiritually alert than ever before so I can do the greatest good for Your Kingdom in this hour, in Jesus' name. Amen.

Ephesians 5:14

—————— CONFESSION ——————

I am spiritually, physically and mentally
alert to the leading of the Holy Spirit,
and I am obedient to His voice.

Heavenly Father, I accept the commission Jesus gave to go into all the world to preach the Gospel to every person. Guide me in adequate preparation in the natural and in the Spirit to assume this responsibility, Lord. You said that signs would follow the teaching of Your Word: Casting out devils; speaking in new tongues; taking authority over every work of the devil; and laying hands on the sick so they will recover. In Jesus' name, these signs will follow me in my own household, in my neighborhood, in my work place, in the marketplace and to the ends of my world – wherever You take me, Lord! Hallelujah!

Mark 16:15-20

———————————— C O N F E S S I O N ————————————

Jesus Christ confirms the Word I share with
others with signs following. (Mark 16:20.)

Heavenly Father, I am a laborer in Your harvest of souls. You said I would walk as a lamb among wolves. Thank You for giving me divine strategies to win the lost for Your inheritance, Lord, and to outsmart the schemes of the devil.  You will take care of my needs, for You said I am worthy of my hire. As I fully trust You, whether it is in an actual ministry position or as Your ambassador who touches people one on one, You will provide a "more than enough" paycheck, in Jesus' name. Amen.

Luke 10:2-7

———————— CONFESSION ————————

God is the all-sufficient One, El Shaddai, to me!

Father, in Jesus' name, You are the Great Reconciler! Of marriages! Of children! Of families! Of brothers and sisters in You! Of all relationships! With Your help, Father, I will go to the person (or persons) with whom I have had difficulties. I will walk in Your love, humble myself and ask for forgiveness regardless of who was at fault, so the relationship can be restored and the breach mended. I will do it in obedience to Your Word and for Your glory, Lord Jesus. Amen.

Matthew 5:23,24

―――――――――― C O N F E S S I O N ――――――――――

*The Repairer of Breaches in relationships
is working on my behalf!*

Father God, You are Abba Father to me because You have adopted me into Your family! Not only am I Your child, but I am an heir with You and a joint-heir with Jesus Christ. I have free access now to the full inheritance which You have provided. Thank You for delivering me from the bondage of fear and placing me in the arena of faith. Like Abraham, I am learning to call those things forth that are not into existence. As a result, they are manifesting to further the work of Your Kingdom in the earth, in Jesus' name. Amen.

Romans 4:17; Romans 8:15-17

———— CONFESSION ————

What God has promised me,
He will perform! (Rom. 4:21.)

 Father, You said to obey and submit to those who have the rule over me, for You hold them responsible for watching over my soul. They are accountable to You for taking proper care of me. Teach me, Lord, how to treat those in authority over me with honor and respect. Teach me to pray for them so they will represent You well in their position, just as You want me to represent You well in my subservience to them. Teach me how to relate appropriately, contributing to a joyous relationship – one that brings the highest level of productivity, in Jesus' name. Amen.

Hebrews 13:17

—————————— CONFESSION ——————————

I will treat others the way I want to be treated. (Matt. 7:12.)

Heavenly Father, thank You for your divine protection which encompasses the ones I love and care for. You said that it is because of Your mercies that we are not consumed. Your compassions fail not, for they are new every morning. You also said, Father, that you preserve the souls of Your saints, and whoever obeys You shall dwell in safety. Thank You, Father God, for safety for my family, friends and loved ones, in Jesus' name. Amen.

Psalm 97:10; Proverbs 1:33; Lamentations 3:22,23

—— C O N F E S S I O N ——

The Lord preserves my going out and my coming
in now and forevermore. He also preserves the going out
and coming in of my loved ones and friends! (Ps. 121:8.)

Father, it's not always convenient and comfortable to love those who are my enemies! You have not asked me to be someone's carpet to walk on. But I will bless those who curse me. I will do good to those who hate me. And I will pray for those who despitefully use me. I will respond unlike the world, but as You would react, Lord. Thank You, Father, for helping me with all of my "reactions," in Jesus' name. Amen.

Matthew 5:43-48

—————————— CONFESSION ——————————

Another person's actions have no effect upon my reactions.
I will react in all situations as Jesus would,
using The Book as my guide!

Father God, I will remember the poor, not just so You will deliver me in time of trouble, but because Your compassion dominates my heart. You said giving unto the poor is a key to my deliverance from the will of my enemies, Lord. With Your guidance, I will help to meet their spiritual needs as well as their natural needs. To put Your Word in their hearts is like teaching them to fish so they will never lack again. In Jesus' name, help me to be a lifter of others. Amen.

Psalm 41:1,2

——————————— C O N F E S S I O N ———————————

Just as God is the lifter of my head, I will follow His example
and be a lifter of others, causing their lives to be enriched
both spiritually and naturally! (Ps. 3:3.)

Father, in Jesus' name, thank You for bringing a balance to my life. Though most believers, including me, are aware of generational curses which can be broken, we have been taught very little about generational blessings, which are just as real! In the name of Jesus, I break every generational curse upon me and my seed. And Father, I loose the generational blessings from my ancestors who dearly loved You and obeyed Your commands, that our lives may be enriched, in Jesus' name. Amen.

Numbers 14:18

——————————— CONFESSION ———————————

I am flourishing spiritually
because of generational blessings!

Father, You sent Jesus Christ to bear grief and sorrow in my behalf. You sent Him to bear sickness and disease so they wouldn't touch me. You sent Him to bear sin and its penalty so I could be free of it. You sent Jesus to intercept calamities and tragedies so they would not come near me or any member of my household. I will not be afflicted with any of the devil's oppressions in Jesus' name. Instead, I will walk in wholeness of spirit, body and soul. Hallelujah!

Isaiah 53:3-5

—————————— C O N F E S S I O N ——————————

I am the healed of the Lord in spirit, body and soul!

Father, Your Word is like a sword, quick and powerful. Your Word cuts through the works of the flesh and of darkness and clears the way for the light of Your love to shine through! Your Word spoken from my lips – the rhema word – works as a sword, discerning right from wrong, truth from lies and deceit, and sets my feet upon a highway of new life, in Jesus' name. Amen.

Hebrews 4:12

―――――――――― CONFESSION ――――――――――

*I will judge myself by the Word of God
so that no man will judge me. (1 Cor. 2:15.)*

Heavenly Father, You said in Your Word that I am to remember how You brought the Israelites out from the bondage of Pharaoh and the Egyptians, representative of the devil. Your outstretched arm is still at work for me, Father!  I'll not be put to shame by the enemy. Instead, You will exalt me in the presence of my enemies, in Jesus' name. Amen.

Deuteronomy 7:18-23

———————— C O N F E S S I O N ————————

*God is a mighty God to me! He will deliver
my enemies into my hand!*

Heavenly Father, You have indicated in Your Word that it is good and pleasant to You for Your Body of believers to dwell together in unity. Then, as we come together in groups of two or more in Your name, Lord Jesus, You said You would be in our midst. You also said that anything we agree upon that is in line with Your will, it will be done for us by our Father God! In the name of Jesus, cleanse me and purify me so I will be a contributor to the unity of the entire Body of Christ. Amen.

Psalm 133:1-3 AMP; Matthew 18:19,20

———————— C O N F E S S I O N ————————

*Nothing is impossible to me as I walk in
one accord with the Body of Christ.*

Heavenly Father, thank You for the examples You gave us from the lives of Paul and Timothy of how we are to live. Even though they were ministers of the Gospel, they labored day and night so as not to take from other people for their daily needs of food, clothing and shelter. Paul commanded the people, "If any would not work, neither should he eat." Paul said it was Your command, Father, that in quietness we are to work and eat our own bread. Help me, in the name of Jesus, to walk and live in the divine order which You have ordained, Father. Amen.

2 Thessalonians 3:7-12

—————————— CONFESSION ——————————

I am diligent in working to provide
for the needs of my own household.

Father, in Jesus' name, I am feeding myself with the spiritual diet of Your Word. I eat spiritually on a regular basis, just as I do physically. Your Word will go forth out of my mouth. It will not return unto me void, but it will accomplish that which You intend. Thank You for giving me revelation of Your Word, Lord. The spoken (rhema) Word will cause prosperity to every area of my life, in Jesus' name. Amen.

Isaiah 55:11

———————— CONFESSION ————————

Because I love and obey God's Word,
I am giving a spiritual legacy to my seed.

Father, You demonstrated Your power through Moses, as he obeyed You and stretched out the rod. It caused the Red Sea to part so Your people could be delivered from their enemies into a place of safety. You dried up the waters of the Jordan River so Joshua could lead the Israelites to a safe place prepared for them. You are the same yesterday, today and forever! Thank You for doing whatever needs to be done, not only to deliver me from my enemies, but to keep me running with Your vision without being hindered or delayed, in Jesus' name. Amen.

Joshua 4:23,24; Hebrews 13:8

———————————— C O N F E S S I O N ————————————

Jesus Christ is preserving me today from all
of the works of the enemy!

Father God, You are alive! I bless and exalt You in Jesus' name. Thank You for avenging me and delivering me from my enemies. You always lift me high above those who rise up against me. I have nothing to fear from those who oppose me wrongfully, for You are on my side. Praise You, Father, in Jesus' name.

2 Samuel 22:47-51

———————— C O N F E S S I O N ————————

The enemy has already been crushed beneath my feet!

Heavenly Father, You said for Your Word to come to full fruition in my life, I must mix faith with it and not just hear it. The faith principle is believing and speaking Your Word. You have asked me to become a doer of Your Word.  The Spirit of God through James said that faith without works (or being a doer of the Word) is like the physical body without the spirit. When the spirit leaves the body, the physical body is dead. Teach me to put feet to my faith, Lord Jesus, for I want to be fully alive while I yet live!! Amen.

Hebrews 4:2; James 2:26

———————————— CONFESSION ————————————

My faith is growing continually as I hear the Word of God repeatedly. (Rom. 10:17.)

Father, it's apparent that David needed a divine strategy for recovering his wives and children, taken captive after the Amalekites burned his hometown of Ziklag! Though he was greatly distressed, he encouraged himself in You, Lord. You gave him the plan and the word to recover all: pursue! My answers and strategies for everything I face are in You, Lord. I will encourage myself in You, for You will never fail me. You will bring me through any circumstance, not down under, but on top! I will recover all the enemy has taken from me, in Jesus' name. Amen.

1 Samuel 30:1-8

———————————— CONFESSION ————————————

With God's strategies operating in me by His Spirit,
I will win in every situation that comes my way!

Heavenly Father, You said that if any man would serve You, they should follow You. I will follow You, Lord, and I want You to be glorified in the work You have created for me to do. You have chosen me to bring forth fruit that should remain for Your Kingdom. Help me, Holy Spirit, to bring forth fruit in the position of employment in which I have been placed. I will obey my earthly master, and I will work for him as if I am working for You, Lord. Help me to be a diligent, loyal and dependable employee, in Jesus' name. Amen.

John 12:25,26; John 15:16; Colossians 3:22,23

——————— C O N F E S S I O N ———————

I will provide well for my own household
spiritually and naturally. They shall not lack
any good thing. (1 Tim. 5:8; Ps. 84:11.)

Father God, thank You for the privilege to serve You with my life. Because of the enablement of the Holy Spirit, I am instant in season and out of season to testify of Your goodness. I will reprove, rebuke and exhort with love, kindness and truth in Jesus' name. I will lift and not condemn. I will encourage, which will drive out hopelessness. I will speak truth, which will drive out despair. Hallelujah!

2 Timothy 4:2

———————————————— C O N F E S S I O N ————————————————

My hope and expectation are in the Lord!
(Ps. 39:7 AMP.)

Father, because of Your instruction and love, I am prepared to be a teacher, living on a diet of the strong meat of Your Word, made skillful in the word of righteousness. I am not a baby who is still on a diet of milk. Though I am a teacher, I am yet teachable. Though I am a leader, I am still learning. Though I am a champion, I am still being transformed into Your image and likeness. Thank You for Your indescribable love and care of me, in Jesus' name. Amen.

Hebrews 5:12-14

CONFESSION

I am being filled with the Spirit of wisdom and revelation in the knowledge of God. (Eph. 1:17.)

Heavenly Father, You have given me Your Word as an example to follow. You shared how Enoch was translated and never saw death. His testimony was that he *pleased* You! I want to please You, Lord, with a heart that is perfect toward You. With actions and words that are perfect toward others. With motives that are unquestionable by You or by man. My highest goal is to be just like You, Lord Jesus! Amen.

Hebrews 11:5

― CONFESSION ―

Each day I am maturing and being perfected
in the Lord to a greater degree than the day before!

According to Your Word, Father God, my actions of courage can cause someone to inherit the land (the marriage, the relationships, the health and healing, the deliverance and provision, for example) You have promised them. Then, it is also true that my lack of courage to act upon Your Word could cause someone to fail to enter into their promised land. Help me, Lord Jesus, to function as a spark plug to faith, causing other people, even competitors in the natural, to succeed in what You have called them to do. What I plant in someone else's success will come back to me, in Jesus' name. Amen.

Deuteronomy 31:7,8

——————————— C O N F E S S I O N ———————————

I'll not cower, shrink back, fear, tremble, or flinch
from any situation. I'll face it head on with the sword
of the Word in my mouth and overcome it!

Heavenly Father, I am filled with the knowledge of Your will in all wisdom and spiritual understanding. Your will and Your Word are one and the same. Your Word gives me direction in how to walk worthy of You. It guides me in how to be fruitful in every good work. It increases my knowledge of You, and strengthens me with Your might. In You, Lord Jesus, I am patient and longsuffering with joyfulness. Thank You, Father, for providing for me in great liberality through the inheritance made available to me in Jesus Christ. Amen.

Colossians 1:9-12

—————————— C O N F E S S I O N ——————————

I have been redeemed from the old life of darkness
and translated into the Kingdom of God's dear Son
through the shed blood of Jesus Christ! (Col. 1:13,14.)

Father, I am obedient to those in authority over me -- spiritual leaders, parents or guardians, employers and supervisors. Help me to submit to their leadership with an appropriate attitude. You have called them to accountability over my soul. In the name of Jesus, I will represent You well, Father, as a submissive servant and laborer in You. Instead of being critical of those in authority over me, I will pray for them, speaking Your Word over them, Father, in Jesus' name. Amen.

Titus 2:9; Hebrews 13:17

———————— CONFESSION ————————

With my words and actions,
I will bless those in authority over me.

Father, You said in Your Word that the person who does not provide for his own, especially for those of his own household, has denied the faith and is worse than an unbeliever. Help me to take care of those in my household, Lord, and then reach beyond my own to the household of faith! I ask, Father, that the household of each godly ministry, from leadership down through the ranks, have the attitude, "What can I do to bless this individual and enhance his/her walk with You, Lord?" I submit to the Holy Spirit for an adjustment on my attitude, in Jesus' name. Amen.

1 Timothy 5:8

———————————— CONFESSION ————————————

The Holy Spirit is adjusting my attitude today
to be like that of my Heavenly Father!

Father, it is Your command that I increase more and more in the knowledge of You and in walking out this knowledge in practical, everyday living. I will study to be quiet, to do my own business and work with my own hands as You have commanded. Lord Jesus, I will walk in honesty toward every person. Because of Your provision, I will have lack of nothing! Thank You for Your abundance which You are showering upon me! Amen.

Col. 1:9-10; 1 Tim. 2:2; 1 Thess. 4:12

―――――― CONFESSION ――――――

*God equips me and provides me
with everything I need to carry out His will.*

Father, You said that because the Holy Spirit is a Spirit of truth, He will guide me into all truth. He will lift You up, Lord Jesus. Whatever He hears from You, Father, He will make known to me. He will show me things to come. Thank You, Father, for making me wiser than the children of the world – all because of the Holy Spirit's activities in my life and His freedom to function in and through me, in Jesus' name. Amen.

John 16:13

———————— CONFESSION ————————

The Spirit of truth Who lives in me will reveal that which is false, deceitful and counterfeit.

Lord Jesus, help me to bring a healthy balance between natural work that I must accomplish and a time of spiritual devotion to develop my relationship with You. Cleanse my heart from anxiety, Lord, that would interrupt my thoughts of You or my time with You. Though I know You want me to be neat, orderly and diligent, You also want me to pursue the things that will never be taken away from me in this life or in the next! That's time with You, Lord, in the Word, in fasting and in prayer to seek You. I love You, Lord, more than anything else, in Jesus' name. Amen.

Luke 10:38-42

—— CONFESSION ——

*I will not allow my time alone with the Lord to be
interrupted with wrong thoughts or needless activities.
I will let God bring an appropriate balance.*

Father, You anointed Your own Son, Jesus Christ, with the Holy Ghost and power for ministry. Though I may never stand in a pulpit, I receive the anointing of the Holy Spirit and power to be an ambassador for You – in my own neighborhood, office, business, school, City Hall, state legislature, in the Halls of Congress and other government offices, wherever You place me. I want to be a channel of deliverance and healing to those oppressed by the devil, in Jesus' name. Amen.

Mark 16:17,18; Acts 10:38

CONFESSION

I am an ambassador of the Lord Jesus Christ, and I have been reconciled to God. God hath made Him to be sin for us, who knew no sin, that we might be made the righteousness of God in Him. (2 Cor. 5:20,21.)

Father God, You are mighty in the midst of me! I shall not be afraid, nor shall I be slack at the tasks You have assigned to me in Jesus' name. Thank You for saving me. Thank You for rejoicing over me with great joy and singing! I receive Your promise, Lord, that You will also bring praise and fame to me where I have been put to shame, regardless of who was at fault. Thank You for turning my captivity, Lord, and allowing me to live for You! Hallelujah!

Zephaniah 3:14-20

----------- CONFESSION -----------

My lips are filled with praise and worship to the Lord,
the Mighty One in the midst of me!

Father, I need a refresher course and a tuneup on the words that come forth from me! You said that foul or polluting language, evil words, or unwholesome or worthless talk should never come out of my mouth. Help me to think and speak only that which is good and beneficial to the spiritual progress of others. I yield to Your adjustments and corrections, Lord Jesus! Amen.

Ephesians 4:29 AMP

——————————— C O N F E S S I O N ———————————

Today, I will please the Holy Spirit
with my thoughts, words and actions!

Heavenly Father, cleanse my heart and my tongue for the good words You would have me speak over others. You have commanded in Your Word that I not speak evil of any person, regardless of what they have done. You have not called me to judgment but to prayer! As I think of the person who has come against me, Lord, I release and forgive him/her. I call this person blessed. I call the emptiness in his/her heart to be filled with Your joy and love. My own tongue will no longer hold me in captivity because of speaking negative, unkind words or judgments over others in Jesus' name. Amen.

Titus 3:2; James 3:10

———————— C O N F E S S I O N ————————

In my tongue is life and not death,
blessing and not cursing! (Prov. 18:21.)

Father, in my spirit, I hear the sound of abundance of the rain of Your Spirit! Elijah heard the sound of rain when there had been a drought for three and a half years. As Your prophet, Lord, he prayed and spoke the rain into existence, and it manifested in abundance. Help me to be like Elijah, Father – a creator with my words, rich in faith, so in tune with Your Spirit that I know, at least in part, the events that are about to take place. In the name of Jesus, I ask that my lifestyle be a demonstration of Your creativity and power, Father! Amen.

1 Kings 18:41-46

———————————— C O N F E S S I O N ————————————

The rain of the Spirit is causing
a new revival in my own heart!

Father God, I will not fear, for Jesus said it is Your good pleasure to give me Your Kingdom. That means You desire that I enjoy Your grace, mercy and provision now in this life, so I can literally have heaven on earth – in my home, marriage and family, in all relationships, in the work place and in the marketplace! Everywhere! Father, rid me of any poverty thinking in Jesus' name, for I will maintain a mentality of heavenly provision! With Your provision, I will bring heaven on earth to others' lives in the now! Hallelujah!

Luke 12:31,32

————————— CONFESSION —————————

I have set my heart to not only give of God's best
to others, but to enjoy His best in my own life!

Father, as an "add on" to the refresher course and tuneup on my words, help me to grow in the area of faith-filled words in Jesus' name. Paul said his speech and preaching were "not with enticing words of man's wisdom, but *in demonstration of the Spirit and of power.*" Holy Spirit, convict me should I speak fear-filled words, because I want to remove them from my vocabulary! Reassure me when I am speaking faith-filled words which will bring the power of God on the scene! Hallelujah!

1 Corinthians 2:4,5

—————————— C O N F E S S I O N ——————————

Daily, I am filling my heart with God's Word,
for it is out of the abundance of my heart
that my mouth speaks. (Matt. 12:34.)

Heavenly Father, thank You for the Holy Spirit Who is walking me step by step into the completion of the destiny to which You have called me! Thank You for blessing me richly along the way with great cities I did not build; houses full of all good things; wells I did not dig; and vineyards I did not plant. I will not forget, Lord, that it was You Who brought me out of bondage! Amen.

Deuteronomy 6:10-13

——————— C O N F E S S I O N ———————

I am a living memorial to show that the Lord
is upright and faithful to His promises. (Ps. 92:15 AMP.)

Heavenly Father, help me to praise You in the midst of natural circumstances (not for them, but in them), for praise will break the bands of wickedness off of me. Just as Paul and Silas praised You in a situation of natural, illegal imprisonment and You loosed their bands, You will do the same for me. As I move in Your principles and by Your Spirit, there is nothing the enemy can do to bind my heart and mind. I am totally free in You, Lord Jesus, regardless of natural circumstances! Hallelujah!

Acts 16:17-39

——————————— CONFESSION ———————————

Because Jesus Christ has set me free,
I am free indeed!

Father, I will stir up the gift You have placed within me. It will no longer lay dormant and neglected as a hope deferred, but I will arise with a spirit of power, love and a sound mind. You have not given me a spirit of fear, so I will boldly pursue the development and use of Your gift within me. I will follow the Holy Spirit's leading, knowing that my gift will make room for me and bring me before great men. Hallelujah!

Proverbs 13:12; Proverbs 18:19; 1 Timothy 4:14; 2 Timothy 1:6,7

--- CONFESSION ---

God's gift within me is maturing for the purpose of blessing mankind with witty inventions that will enrich their natural and spiritual lives!

Father God, You are worthy of all praise. I will praise You for Your mighty acts, according to Your excellent greatness. I will praise You in the sanctuary with instruments and with the dance; with stringed instruments and organs; with cymbals and high sounding cymbals. As long as I have breath, I will praise You, Father God, in Jesus' holy name. You are a mighty God to me! Hallelujah!

Psalm 150:1-6

——————————— C O N F E S S I O N ———————————

I will praise the Lord each day, not for what praise
will do for me, but because I simply love and adore Him!

Heavenly Father, You said I can have hope in the face of the physical death of a loved one. Just as Your Son arose from the grave and became the Resurrection and the Life, He has given this same manner of life to every believer. Homegoing of a loved one is a time of great celebration, because the spirit of the person immediately comes into Your presence, Lord Jesus. You said that whoever believes in You will never die. Thank You for the perfectness of Your great love, Lord Jesus! Amen.

John 11:25,26; 1 Thessalonians 4:13-18

—————————— CONFESSION ——————————

God created me a three-part being: spirit, soul and body.
My spirit man goes into His presence at physical death.
Whether in life or in death, He never leaves me!

Lord Jesus, You said that Your grace is sufficient for me in any situation, particularly where the enemy is buffeting to hinder Your work through me. It is not Satan who will keep my heart humbled before You, Lord. It is a decision of my own will to walk in continual humility of heart in my actions and attitude before You. It is a decision of my will to obey Your Word. I choose to bring honor and glory to Your name, because the devil's buffeting cannot prevail, in Jesus' name. Amen.

2 Corinthians 12:9

--------- CONFESSION ---------

God's grace is more than sufficient for any challenge I face! I'll not cower or weaken by any attack of the enemy, but I will quickly sail through it because the Greater One dominates me!

Father, I need Your help to learn how to handle persecution without it touching my spirit man. You said persecutions would come. You also said I am blessed for being reviled (spoken against with harsh language) and spoken evil of falsely. With Your help, Lord, when I find myself in this situation, I will rejoice and be glad, because You were persecuted in the same manner. Thank You for helping me to be like You, Lord Jesus! Hallelujah!

Matthew 5:10-12

CONFESSION

Jesus Christ overcame the world and its tribulation and troubles. Because He lives in me and I am seated with Him in heavenly places, I, too, have overcome the world!

Heavenly Father, when the enemy pursued the Israelites, You gave a word to Moses, their leader, which is a word that is just as alive for me today: "Fear ye not, stand still, and see the salvation of the Lord...the Egyptians [enemies] whom ye have seen today, ye shall see them again no more for ever. The Lord shall fight for you, and ye shall hold your peace." Lord, You are fighting for me because I have fully committed myself to the life and walk of the Spirit. Fear is what fights faith, and faith is what takes a champion to the finish line! In You, Lord Jesus, I am free of fear and empowered with unlimited faith! Hallelujah!

Exodus 14:13,14

———— CONFESSION ————

The enemy cannot prevail against me, and my circumstances will be changed for good because God is fighting for me!

Thank You, Lord Jesus, for choosing me and ordaining me to bring forth fruit that will remain — the eternal fruit of Your Spirit. I am Your servant, but You no longer call me a servant. You call me Your friend, because You reveal to me everything You hear from the Father. It is because of my relationship with You, Lord Jesus, that I am given secrets made known to You by the Father that cause me to excel in this life. I'll never be "down under" in my walk with You! But because You live in me, I will always be "at the top" for the glory of the Father! Hallelujah!

John 15:15,16

------------------ CONFESSION ------------------

Jesus treats me as a long-revered friend.
I am His friend, and He is mine!

Thank You, Father God, that You are teaching me to profit. You are leading me in the way I should go. My obedience to go where You want me to go and do what You want me to do sets the stage for divine prosperity in Jesus' name. I receive Your prosperity in spirit, soul and body, Lord, that I might never tire physically or mentally, lack spiritually or weaken in the championship run to which You have called me! Aging in the natural will not affect my performance! In fact, I will simply speed up, because I am divinely energized! Hallelujah!

Isaiah 48:17

—— CONFESSION ——

Today I am walking out God's plan for me!

Heavenly Father, there are times when I have suffered from the pain and anguish of a broken heart. As I have turned to You to lead me through the situation, You have delivered me from pain and sorrow and healed my wounds. It didn't all happen in one day, but layer by layer the wounds were completely healed. Father, remove any brokenness from me, for the new friendships and relationships cannot be what You want them to be without full healing in the hearts of those involved. I yield to Your healing power, in Jesus' name. Amen.

Psalm 34:18; Psalm 147:3; Luke 4:18

─────────── C O N F E S S I O N ───────────

I refuse to carry the wounds, pains and sorrows
of a broken heart, for Jesus Christ already paid for total
healing for me — spirit, body and soul!

Father God, You have given me the tongue of the learned and the ear of the learned. I will know what to speak to someone who is weary at the time appointed by You, in Jesus' name. I will awake each morning with the ear of the learned, which will cause me to walk, not in the way of rebellion, but in the way the Spirit leads. I have set my face like a flint to know Your ways, Lord, so I will never be brought to shame or confounded. Instead, I will bring great glory to Your Kingdom, in the name of Jesus. Amen.

Isaiah 50:4-7

—————————— C O N F E S S I O N ——————————

*I will trust in the name and in the
shed blood of the Lord Jesus Christ!*

Lord Jesus, the words You spoke to Paul are just as alive to Your children today: "Rise, stand upon your feet, for I have appeared unto you to make you a minister and a witness of the things which you have seen, and of the things which I will yet reveal to you." I accept Your call, Lord, to share that which You have imparted to me to pull people from the highway headed to hell to the highway headed to Heaven! Amen.

Acts 26:16-18

———————————— CONFESSION ————————————

The Spirit of the Lord is upon me, because he hath anointed me to preach the gospel to the poor; he hath sent me to heal the brokenhearted, to preach deliverance to the captives, and recovering of sight to the blind, to set at liberty them that are bruised. (Luke 4:18.)

Father, You said in Your Word that it is difficult for the person who "trusts" in riches to enter Your Kingdom. You also said that it is the love of money that is the root of all evil. I will not allow covetousness, an unhealthy drive or lust for money, to open up a ditch of error and sorrow in which to fall. I am a wise steward of the finances You give to me, Lord. I will use them to further Your Kingdom in the special ways to which You have called me, in Jesus' name. Amen.

Mark 10:24; 1 Timothy 6:10

—————————— CONFESSION ——————————

Money itself is not evil. I will use it as the blessing
God means for it to be, without it getting a grip on me.

Father, the word You gave to Solomon at the completion of the building of Your temple is a word for my life, business, career and ministry. "If thou wilt walk before me...in integrity of heart, and in uprightness, to do according to all that I have commanded thee, and wilt keep my statutes and my judgments: then I will establish the throne of thy kingdom...." My life and its outreach are established upon You, Lord. I will be successful beyond anything the world has to offer, for I will keep each of Your commandments, with the Holy Spirit as my empowerment and guide! Hallelujah!

1 Kings 9:1-5

———————— CONFESSION ————————

*Success in this life for me is assured
because I am established in God.*

Heavenly Father, You have cautioned me not to use the strength of a multitude of horses and chariots for help rather than look to You. In other words, You are asking me not to turn to natural man and the flesh for counsel. But it is Your plan that I turn to Your Spirit for help and guidance, which You have provided. Lord Jesus, I will trust in You and in the Holy Spirit. I will not put my confidence in man, in Jesus' name. Amen.

Isaiah 31:1-3; Philippians 3:3

———————— CONFESSION ————————

My trust is in the Lord. He is my confidence.
He will unveil to me His strategies for success
in every situation! (Prov. 3:26.)

Heavenly Father, when I pass through the waters of persecution and trials, You will be with me. When the rivers of adversity come at me, they will not drown me. When I walk through the fire of Satan's fiery darts, the flames won't touch me and I'll not be burned. You, O Lord, are the Holy One of Israel, my God and my Savior! In You alone I can trust, for You will never fail me, in Jesus' name. Amen.

Isaiah 43:1-3

CONFESSION

The persecutions, trials and troubles I face today are temporary. God's promises of success are permanent, and they prevail in my life!

Heavenly Father, You said that I would not drink again from the cup of trembling and fury, but You have placed this cup into the hands of those who afflict me. Because I accept the completed work of Jesus at Calvary, You are causing me to drink of the new wine of the Holy Spirit. I have received power to be a witness because the Holy Ghost is come upon me, in Jesus' name. Amen.

Isaiah 51:22,23; Acts 1:8

——————————— CONFESSION ———————————

*The love of God is shed abroad in my heart
by the Holy Spirit. The agape love
of Christ never fails. (Rom. 5:5; 1 Cor. 13:8.)*

Father, You said in Your Word that Daniel, the man with the excellent spirit and in right standing with You, waited in fastings and prayers for three full weeks (or 21 days) for Your answer to his prayers. The vision containing the answer was delayed because of the warfare withstanding the angel who was sent with the answer. The angel said to Daniel, "I have come for thy words." Thank You, Father, that the moment I pray, Your answer is on its way to me. I will persevere, because the warfare of the devil's forces cannot withstand the heavenly forces sent on my behalf, in Jesus' name. Hallelujah!

Daniel 10:1-13

——————— C O N F E S S I O N ———————

God's angels always break through the satanic forces
that are sent to withstand me, because my words
are in agreement with God's Word.

Heavenly Father, help me to grow in my trust of You so that I will not waver in faith – in believing, speaking and trusting in the fulfillment of Your Word in my life. I do not want to be a double-minded person, because You said such a person is unstable and will receive nothing of You. When the storms of life rage, Lord, I will believe Your Word above the storms. The storms will then have to submit to the truth of Your Word! They will not be able to prevail against faith in Your Word! Hallelujah!

Hebrews 10:23; James 1:6-8

—————————— CONFESSION ——————————

Because God is faithful, I will hold fast
to the confession of His Word without wavering.

Heavenly Father, You said in Your Word that "the seed of the righteous shall be delivered." Thank You, Father, that You have already delivered my children from the works of the enemy, and great is their peace. Though a thousand may fall at their side and ten thousand at their right hand, they will not be touched. Thank You for giving Your angels charge over them, to guard, protect and keep them in all of their ways. No evil or plague will come to my children. Because they honor You, Lord, and honor us as their parents [or guardians], it is well with them, in Jesus' name. Amen.

Psalm 91:1,4,7,10-12; Proverbs 11:21; Isaiah 54:13; Ephesians 6:1-4

―――――――――― CONFESSION ――――――――――

My children have been trained in the way they should go. They have been filled with the wisdom of God's Word, which will guide them and keep them spiritually alert! (Prov. 22:6.)

Thank You, Father, that You go before me as a consuming fire. You route the enemy and destroy him before me, not because of my righteousness, but because of Your goodness! Lord Jesus, cleanse me so I will never be categorized as a "stiff-necked" person, doing my own thing. Help me always to be teachable and pliable in Your hands, Lord. When I taste of success, help me to remain teachable, pliable and humble, in Jesus' holy name. Amen.

Deuteronomy 9:3-7

——————— CONFESSION ———————

The consuming fire of the Lord that goes before me
clears a path of peace, safety and abundance
on which I'll walk today!

Heavenly Father, thank You for the help and guidance of the Holy Spirit! I have made a decision that I'll not be a contributor to strife or a participant in it at any cost. It is an open door for confusion and every evil work. I will esteem others as better than myself. I will look to You, Lord Jesus, and ask what You would have me to do when there is an opportunity for strife. I will avoid it and kill it, closing the doors to the enemy, in Jesus' name. Amen.

Philippians 2:3

──────────── C O N F E S S I O N ────────────

I am a peacemaker and a strife killer!

Heavenly Father, there is a new song in my heart today. I will praise You to the ends of the earth and make known Your goodness and faithfulness. Up until this moment in time, everything concerning me that took place is classed as "former things." You said the former things are passed, and You will now do a new thing, Lord. Thank You for revealing to me the new thing that You have planned for my life. I will step into it and bring the glory and honor of it unto You, in Jesus' name. Amen.

Isaiah 42:8-10

——————————— CONFESSION ———————————

I am walking in the fullness of God's new plans for me!

Heavenly Father, thank You for revealing to me in Your Word that tithing wasn't just an Old Testament law. It is also a New Testament principle for financial increase. The firstfruits, the tithe, or the first tenth of my time as well as my income belong to You, Lord. In fact, all I have belongs to You. In Jesus' name, help me to be a wise steward, not only of the tithe, but of all that You give me, Lord. Amen.

Deuteronomy 14:22; Malachi 3:7-12; Luke 18:12

——————— C O N F E S S I O N ———————

I am the steward, not the owner, of all that God
entrusts to me. I am a wise steward,
bringing honor and glory to God!

Father, after many years of turbulence as a result of rebellion, Your grace covered and You brought the Israelites into a place of victory and rest. Every Word You had spoken to them came to pass while they were under Joshua's leadership. Regardless of my past, or the past of any other believer who is committed to You, Father, You are bringing us into great victories in this hour. Every Word You have spoken is manifesting just as You said it would. Thank You, Father, for Your faithfulness, in Jesus' name. Amen.

Joshua 21:45

— CONFESSION —

I forget those things which are behind and reach for those things which are before. I press toward the mark for the prize of the high calling of God in Christ Jesus. (Phil. 4:13,14.)

Father, You said in Your Word that divorce in marriage results from the hardness of a person's heart. I am asking You this day to plow up the soil of my heart, Lord, so that my heart does not become hardened in my dealings with my mate – or so it does not become hardened, causing me to make the wrong choices even in business affairs or friendship relationships. What You have joined together, I will protect, Father, in my own life. I will also stand in the gap to protect the marriage covenant of others, in Jesus' name. Amen.

Mark 10:1-9

CONFESSION

I am yielded to the continual work of the Holy Spirit,
Who will keep my heart tender before God.

Heavenly Father, thank You for Your direction in every matter that concerns me. You said if I will listen to Your Spirit, You will speak, "This is the way, walk ye in it." Help me to be more sensitive to Your Spirit, Lord. Teach me to be obedient to You without "reasoning" out Your directives. I will magnify the words of the Spirit and appropriately judge the advice and counsel of man, in Jesus' name. Amen.

Isaiah 30:21

—————————————— C O N F E S S I O N ——————————————

I will hear and heed the counsel of the Holy Spirit,
for He will keep me out of ditches and on the main road!

Father, thank You for the example Abraham gave to believe You, regardless of how far-fetched in the natural Your promises may seem to be. Because Abraham was fully persuaded that what You spoke You would do, he received the manifestation of Your promises, Lord. There is no room in my life for doubt and unbelief of Your Word, Father. I am maturing in faith to the "fully persuaded" stage, that what You have spoken in Your Word and what You will yet speak to me personally, You will surely perform. Hallelujah!

Romans 4:20,21

———— CONFESSION ————

God's promises are cause for great revelry, for they will not return void. They will be fully performed in my life!

Heavenly Father, You specifically said in Your Word that as Your child, I am to have *no fellowship* with the unfruitful works of darkness. In You, Lord Jesus, I am a child of the light. Darkness has no place in me. I will reprove those who are walking in sin with the truth of Your Word, tempered with Your love, Lord. I will *fellowship* with other believers of like spirit. But I will *witness,* rather than fellowship, to those who are not walking in Your light, in Jesus' name. Amen.

Ephesians 5:11

——————— C O N F E S S I O N ———————

I am walking in the light of God's Word. I'll not let anyone or anything weaken my spiritual commitment and growth.

Father, if there ever was a time for possessing a spirit of faith like the Shunammite woman, it is now! I want to be known as having a spirit like hers, totally undaunted by the severity of natural circumstances – in this case, the death of her only son. She was fearless. She was compassionate and respectful of the man of God, Elisha. She refused to accept the death of her son, but held to Your Word through the prophet. She demanded what was hers – the restoration of her son to life! And she got it! And she gave You praise! Help me to be like her in spirit, Lord Jesus. Amen.

2 Kings 4:8-37

———————————— C O N F E S S I O N ————————————

All is well with me! I will have what God says is mine.
The devil will no longer steal, kill and destroy in my life!

Father, I now realize that there is *absolutely nothing* the enemy can do to hurt me when I am walking in obedience to You. Just as You protected the four Hebrew children, You will protect me. They did not even smell of smoke. The fire in the furnace had no power over them. Not a hair of their heads was singed. In like manner, after Daniel's overnight stay in the lions' den, he was not harmed in any way. The key was that they fully believed in You, Father, and they were in relationship with You. Hallelujah!

Daniel 3:1-27

CONFESSION

Even though I walk through the valley of the shadow of death, I will fear no evil, for You are with me. (Ps. 23:4.)

Father God, forgive me for the times I have been a stone-thrower with my words and unfair judgments of others! When the woman, caught in the act of adultery, was brought to You, You did not condemn. Men under the Law stood ready to stone her to death, but You leaned to the Spirit and said, "He that is without sin among you, let him first cast a stone at her." The accusers disappeared! Teach me to be a lifter and an encourager regardless of man's sin, in Jesus' name. Amen.

John 8:1-11

———————————— C O N F E S S I O N ————————————

I will run from sin and the
very appearance of evil. (1 Thess. 5:22.)

Father, it is spiritually and naturally healthy to be corrected by You, but it's not always fun! I want to grow up in You, Lord, and rise to the highest level possible for You and Your Kingdom! You said, Lord, that whom You love You chasten or discipline, just as a natural parent who loves their child provides guidelines of discipline. In the name of Jesus, I will see Your correction as profitable for my walk of holiness! Amen.

Hebrews 12:5-11

—————————— CONFESSION ——————————

*I accept God's chastening, for it will yield
in me the peaceable fruit of righteousness! (Heb. 12:11.)*

Father, little children are leading many into Your Kingdom in this hour. They are so pliable, tender, loving, teachable and trusting that they are able to break through the hardened hearts of those no one else can seem to reach. I call my children, and the children I know, anointed and blessed to lead many to You in this hour. In Jesus' name, these children will do even greater works than I have done. Glory to God!

Isaiah 8:18; Isaiah 11:6

———————————— CONFESSION ————————————

My children (and the children I know)
are effective fishers of men for God's Kingdom!

Father, help me to be more diligent to pray for kings and for all who are in positions of leadership in the nations of the world – on all levels – local, state and national. Help me to be more diligent in praying for my brothers and sisters in the Body of Christ. You said this is good and acceptable with You, Father. You also said it is the key to a quiet and peaceable life that will be conducted in all godliness and honesty. In the name of Jesus, help me to be more sensitive in my spirit to Your leading in prayer, Holy Spirit. Thank You!

1 Timothy 2:1-4

———————— CONFESSION ————————

I am diligent to pray daily for spiritual and natural
leadership in our land and across the world.

Heavenly Father, thank You for the promise that because I have made Your Son, Jesus Christ, my Lord and Savior, my entire household will be saved. In Jesus' name, I claim the salvation and deliverance of my loves ones. (Call them by name.) Help me to see them saved and serving You. Help me to love and accept them, Lord Jesus, just as You do — without condemnation but with full acceptance! Amen.

Acts 16:31

―――――――――― C O N F E S S I O N ――――――――――

Just as I am accepted in the Beloved, the Lord Jesus Christ, every member of my household is also accepted by Him! (Eph. 1:6.)

Father, help me to be obedient to You in every area of life. You said that rebellion is as the sin of witchcraft and stubbornness is as iniquity and idolatry. Rebellion, stubbornness, or any other attribute of Satan's nature cannot live in me, because I am blood-bought, blood-cleansed and blood-kept in Jesus' name. I am teachable and obedient. I am a reflection of all of Jesus' attributes! Amen.

1 Samuel 15:23

———————— CONFESSION ————————

I overcome challenges, difficulties and opposition with the blood of the Lamb and the word of my testimony! (Rev. 12:11.)

Father, I never want to be one who honors You with my lips, with my heart far from You, caught up in the traditions and doctrines of men. If ideas and doctrines of men do not agree with Your Word, Father, I will reject them, because  Your Word is my standard. It is my Handbook containing the answers for any need or situation I will ever encounter. Your answers will put me over into victory, while man's traditions will ditch me. I'll stay in the middle of the road, with my eyes on You and Your Word, Father, in Jesus' name. Amen.

Mark 7:6-9

———————————— CONFESSION ————————————

I will honor the Word as the highest code
for my behavior and beliefs.

Heavenly Father, I need Your help to grow in patience and hold fast to the confidence I have in You and Your Word. By a quality choice I have made, I will not allow the storms of life that assail me to overcome me. You said, Lord, that after I have done Your will, I will receive the manifestation of Your promises. Do an overhaul on me, Holy Spirit, to strengthen my confidence and to help me be as stable as the Word, which never changes! Hallelujah!

Hebrews 10:35,36

—————————— CONFESSION ——————————

God is orchestrating the delivery schedule
for the manifestation of His promises! His time
is now, so I am expecting a miracle today!

Father, I do believe Your Word. Remove from me any unbelief or doubt about the validity of Your commandments, in Jesus' name. The world's allurements to pull me into sin will not be effective in my life or cause me to be deceived, because the fresh manna of Your Word each day keeps me on target with Your plans, Lord. From my beginning to my end, my steadfast confidence is in You, in Jesus' name. Amen.

Hebrews 3:12-19

CONFESSION

My heart fully believes God's Word. I'll not be moved out of His provision of rest by doubt and unbelief.

 Father, I will give unto my servants (or those under my authority) that which is just and equal, as You have commanded. You also said it is to be done in a way that honors You. In Your eyes, Lord, the color of skin is not a reason for segregation of kindness and compassion. It is no reason for the separation of people into categories of favorite and non-favorite. It is no reason for promotion or demotion. Cleanse me, Lord, from any partiality. Help me to remember that all mankind who has been redeemed has one color of blood – RED – the blood of the Lamb, Jesus Christ! In Him, we are one! Hallelujah!

Colossians 4:1

CONFESSION

God's family is made up of the redeemed of every kindred, tongue, people and nation! (Rev. 5:9.)

Heavenly Father, I want to be led by Your Spirit. Though I didn't know how when I was first born again, I have learned about You through the Word. I am continually learning about Your ways and Your nature, and I want to be like You. Thank You for giving me a servant's heart that will change my attitude toward others to concern and compassion. Thank You for teaching me how to be led by Your Spirit step by step, in Jesus' name. Amen.

Galatians 5:16-26

———————————— CONFESSION ————————————

The works of the flesh can no longer lead me.
They have no part of me, for I am led by God's Spirit.

Lord Jesus, thank You for Your compassion which always says, "I will" to anyone who seeks You. When I am in need of healing, You always say, "I will heal you." When I am facing a need, You always say, "I will provide for you abundantly." When I am faced with responsibilities that overwhelm me, You always say, "I will help you." When I am faced with making a decision and I don't know which way to turn, You always say, "I will give you My wisdom." Thank You, Lord Jesus, for Your willingness, as well as Your ability, to help me. Amen.

Matthew 8:1-4

—————————— CONFESSION ——————————

God knows the plans He has for me, plans
to prosper me and not to harm me,
plans to give me hope and a future. (Jer. 29:11.)

Thank You, Father, that the Son of righteousness arises with healing in His wings on my behalf! Thank You, Lord Jesus, for taking every disease and sickness as my substitute at Calvary so I can walk in wholeness. I will tread down the wicked, causing them to be ashes under the soles of my feet, in Jesus' name. Healed and whole and infused with Holy Ghost power, I will bring Your dominion into my world, Father, in the name of Jesus! Amen.

Isaiah 53:4,5; Malachi 4:2,3; 1 Peter 2:24

———————————— CONFESSION ————————————

God has provided everything I need to cause me to ride on the high places of the earth in health and great success, continually aborting the schemes of the devil.

Heavenly Father, my heart is filled with thanksgiving and praise for the great things You have done for me! I'll not move off course of continually offering to You a sacrifice of praise, for You are worthy of all praise and glory, Lord. Your protocol for prayer is to enter Your presence with thanksgiving. It is to make my requests known to You with thanksgiving. In Jesus' name, I will possess and maintain a thankful heart at all times. Amen.

Psalm 100:4; Philippians 4:6; Hebrews 13:15

CONFESSION

Thanksgiving is in my heart and on my lips. It alleviates perverted vision and replaces it with accurate vision!

Father, You said that I am hidden from the flogging of the tongue, regardless of the source of it. That means destructive words will not pierce my spirit and weaken my effectiveness, in Jesus' name. You also said I am not to be afraid of the destructions and famines in the natural, which will surely come, but I am to laugh at such events, because I am still in Your protective care! Hallelujah! In Jesus' name, there is nothing that can stop me from completing the race set before me, except my own tongue! Thank You for purifying my tongue, Lord! Amen.

Job 5:21,22

—————————— C O N F E S S I O N ——————————

I will go to my grave in a full age, with the assignments completed which God has given me!

Father, You said it's high time to awake out of sleep. The night is far spent, and the day of Jesus' return is at hand. In Jesus' name, I will shake off the complacency, procrastination and comfort of my flesh which have sometimes held me in mediocrity. I will surpass man's standards and accomplishments because I am linked up with You, Lord Jesus. I will deal with others on the basis of Your honesty and integrity. I want Your approval, Lord, rather than the approval of man, in Jesus' name. Amen.

Romans 13:11-14

—————————— CONFESSION ——————————

The diligence, faithfulness, accuracy, compassion
and integrity of the Lord dominate my performance.

Father, because I obey Your Word and am a doer of it, I am like the wise man who built his house upon the rock, as opposed to the foolish man who built his house upon the sand. When the rains, floods and winds of life oppose me, they will not prevail for I will not be moved off of Your Word, Lord. The house whose foundation is not anchored into You and Your Word will be washed away. Victory is assured for me, because my foundation in You is sure, in the name of Jesus. Amen.

Matthew 7:24-27

─────────── CONFESSION ───────────

The foundation of my life is set in the solidified concrete of God's Word!

Father, You put the principles of seed-faith into existence with the giving of Your Son, Jesus Christ, to die for me (and all mankind) so You could, in turn, receive a multiplication of sons and daughters! As I honor You with the firstfruits of my increase, You said my barns would be filled with plenty, which means my checking and savings accounts will be bountiful. You said my presses would burst out with new wine, which refers to the outpouring of Your Spirit. In Jesus' name, help me to be totally obedient to Your supernatural principles, which loose supernatural provision! Hallelujah!

Proverbs 3:9,10; 1 Corinthians 7:23

———————— CONFESSION ————————

As I obey and serve God, His prosperity
and pleasures are loosed unto me. (Job 36:11.)

Heavenly Father, the anointing You have placed upon my life is a permanent anointing. No man can diminish it. No devil can take it from me. I am the only one who can weaken or destroy it through sin and wrongdoing. Thank  You for anointing me with fresh oil so I will be even more productive in Your Kingdom work, which deals with touching the lives of people — healing them, exhorting them, lifting them, encouraging them! In Jesus' name, I will protect the anointing You have given me. Amen.

1 John 2:27

CONFESSION

---

*I am rooted and grounded in the life and love
of the One Who anointed me!*

Father, Your ways are so perfect! You have taught me to tithe and give offerings, not so I'll be religiously strict and proper, but so You can bless me and add fruit to my account! Because the church at Philippi supported Paul faithfully, he spoke of the reward for their sacrifice: "But my God shall supply all your need according to his riches in glory by Christ Jesus." Lord, I will tithe to my local church and plant additional financial seeds and offerings as You direct. I will never lack, for this is one of Your keys for financial prosperity! Hallelujah!

Philippians 4:15-19

———— CONFESSION ————

I will look for ways to be a blessing to someone today!

Heavenly Father, my children are taught by You through the Holy Spirit. Because they are obedient to Your will, they have great peace and undisturbed composure. My children are leaders of leaders because they hear the brush of angels' wings and they respond in faith. They hear Your still, small voice and they believe and obey. They are innocent and impartial. Father, in Jesus' name, help me to be like a child in heart motives and in my responses to You. Amen.

Isaiah 54:13 AMP

——————— C O N F E S S I O N ———————

Like a small child, I am submissive, humble,
obedient and happy to be God's child!

Father, You have indicated in Your Word that it is a serious thing to make a vow and not keep it. This has to do with giving my word and then not being credible to keep it. You said that if I will be faithful to keep my vows, then when I call upon You in the day of trouble, You will keep Your Word to me and deliver me. You have compared the person who makes a vow and doesn't keep it to a "fool," Lord, indicating that You have no pleasure in fools. In the name of Jesus, I will guard my words. When I make a commitment, I will keep it, bringing glory to You, Father! Amen.

Deuteronomy 23:21; Psalm 50:14,15; Ecclesiastes 5:4

———————————— CONFESSION ————————————

The Holy Spirit is the keeper
of the door of my lips! (Ps. 141:3.)

Heavenly Father, I do not desire to be great in the eyes of people, but I do desire to be great in Your estimation of me! You said that David became greater and greater because *You were with him*! It is Your desire to increase and bless me, Father. I want to grow in my relationship with You. As I increase the input of time in meditation of Your Word and in prayer, You will increase in me, Lord Jesus. Hallelujah!

1 Chronicles 11:9 AMP; Psalm 115:14

———————————— C O N F E S S I O N ————————————

I am "on track" with God's standards of growth
for my spiritual life! I am increasing in the
knowledge of Him continually.

Father, You said that even those who are Your children sometimes are destroyed for lack of knowledge of Your Word. I will pursue knowledge of You through Your Word, Father, so I'll never be rejected of You nor will You ever forget my children! I will delight myself in You and in Your Word, Father — not just for the benefits it brings me, but because of a sold-out commitment to You and my love for You, in Jesus' name. Amen.

Psalm 1:2; Hosea 4:6

———————— CONFESSION ————————

The activities of work, as well as pleasure,
of my entire life revolve around my love and
commitment to the Lord Jesus Christ!

Lord Jesus, You said that once I put my hand to the plow — in other words, when I make a full commitment of my life to You — I should not look back and become lukewarm or half-hearted. My focus is upon You, Lord. I will touch as many people as possible with Your life and love today. Continually, I will plow up the soil of people's hearts with Your Word, causing them to be more receptive to You. Amen.

Luke 9:62

—————————— CONFESSION ——————————

I am a laborer in God's harvest fields,
which are white unto harvest. (Matt. 9:37,38.)

 Father, through Paul You said that whatever I do, I am to do it heartily as if I am doing it for You rather than for someone in the natural. As I perform my tasks – at work, at school, at home, in the office, shop, or ministry – as unto You, Lord, I will receive Your reward! Help me to set my heart on serving You with everything I do, Father, for then it also will be acceptable in the natural realm. I will represent You well by representing other people in the same manner, in Jesus' name. Amen.

Colossians 3:23-25

——————————— C O N F E S S I O N ———————————

I will perform my tasks with an attitude of cheerfulness and with diligence and excellence – even the tasks in my own home!

Heavenly Father, as I mature in You, I am learning to cast the challenges that tend to present anxiety, worry and concern upon You more quickly. I'll not carry the heaviness of such, for I wasn't created by You to carry such loads! You created me to carry a light load, Father God. Because of Your affectionate care of me, You said I am to cast the whole of my care upon You once and for all, in Jesus' name. Thank You!

Matthew 11:30; 1 Peter 5:7 AMP

——————————— C O N F E S S I O N ———————————

My yoke is easy, and my burden is light! (Matt. 11:30.)

Father, You said if I don't offend with my words, I am a perfect person. Forgive me for the fires I have started with my own words, Lord. Remove from me a tongue filled with murder and replace it with a tongue of life and love. Remove from me a tongue of belittling and replace it with a tongue of encouragement and uplifting. Remove from me a tongue of cursing and replace it with a tongue of blessing! I submit my tongue to You, Holy Spirit, for a complete makeover! Hallelujah!

James 3:1-10

———————— CONFESSION ————————

With God's help, nothing will leave my tongue
but words that line up with His Word!

Father, You have called me to do even greater works than Jesus did – in healings, miracles, deliverances, teaching, edifying, exhorting and comforting. The only way this is possible is to allow the Holy Spirit to use me completely as He wills. I yield to You, Holy Spirit. Have Your way with me. Thank You for stripping me of the need for man's approval. I'll be bold for You, Lord Jesus! Amen.

John 14:10-12

———————————— C O N F E S S I O N ————————————

Jesus Christ is increasing in me and
my carnal nature is decreasing. (John 3:30.)

Father, You identified anger as sin, and You said not to let the sun go down with anger in my heart toward anyone. Anger gives way to unforgiveness, bitterness and strife, and it gives the devil an open door to me. Through that open door, he is very eager to oblige me with calamities and tragedies. In Jesus' name, I ask You, Father, to root out of me – at my very core – any seeds of anger that have never been dealt with and removed. Cleanse me from the putrefying diseases of bitterness, envy, strife and unforgiveness, in Jesus' name. With this cleansing, the avalanche of Your promised blessings will be unleashed to me! Hallelujah!

Ephesians 4:26,27

———————————— C O N F E S S I O N ————————————

I am cleansed from every characteristic
of an unregenerate life, and Jesus' attributes
are coming into me and flowing through me!

Heavenly Father, thank You for strengthening my inner man with the power and might of Your Spirit. Thank You for dwelling in my heart by faith. Daily, through the work of the Holy Spirit, I am being rooted and grounded more deeply in Your love. It's Your love that makes every other area of life function to the maximum potential. Teach me Your ways of love in dealing with all people, Lord — whether it's with the heathen, my brothers and sisters in the Lord or in the natural, my parents, mate, or children, spiritual or natural leaders, or kings, presidents and world leaders. Thank You!

Ephesians 3:16-21

CONFESSION

Every area of spiritual protocol revolves around
God's love. I am growing in His love.

Father, thank You for Your promise that You will restore *everything* the devil and his cohorts have taken from me. I will never be ashamed, but I will eat in plenty and be satisfied. I will continually praise You, Lord, as You teach me how to resist the devil to the point he can *never* steal, kill, or destroy in any area of my life! You are worthy of all praise, Lord, because You have dealt wondrously with me! Hallelujah!

Joel 2:25-27; John 10:10

———— CONFESSION ————

Because I am anchored into God and led by His Spirit,
I will remain a part of God's special remnant!

Father God, thank You for Your "unspeakable" gift to me and to all humanity who will receive Him – Your Son, Jesus Christ. The gift of Your Son is free, and it is by Your grace, Father, that we receive Him without charge. In exchange for our filth of sin, He makes us pure and holy. In exchange for our unrighteousness, He gives us His righteousness. Father, thank You for the gift of Your Son, Who has made my life complete. Amen.

2 Corinthians 9:15; Ephesians 2:8; 2 Timothy 3:16,17

--------------------- C O N F E S S I O N ---------------------

Jesus Christ, the Lamb of God Who takes away the
sin of the world, redeemed me at the cost of His blood
because of His great love for me! (John 1:29.)

 Father, help me to always give honor to those who are placed in positions of authority over me. I will be obedient to my supervisors in a job situation. I will pray for those in positions of honor in my city, my state and nation. I will honor and pray for my pastor and other spiritual leaders. I will serve my leaders as if I am serving You, Lord Jesus. I'll not find fault and criticize, but I will pray Your Word over them, in Jesus' name. Amen.

———————————— CONFESSION ————————————

As I pray for all people in positions of leadership,
I will lead a quiet and peaceable life
in all godliness and honesty. (1 Tim. 2:2.)

Father, You said in your Word that envy, strife and divisions come from the carnal nature. Forgive me and cleanse me for any involvement in these areas, Lord. I will act out of my spirit man, being perfectly joined together with other members of Your Body. Lord, I will not think of myself more highly than I ought to, but I will think soberly, according as God has dealt to every man the measure of faith, in Jesus' name. Amen.

Romans 12:3; 1 Corinthians 1:10; 1 Corinthians 3:3

————————— C O N F E S S I O N —————————

I will be kindly affectioned to others with brotherly love, in honor preferring others. I will abhor that which is evil and cleave to that which is good. (Rom. 12:9,10.)

Heavenly Father, thank You for helping me to increase and abound in love toward all people. Thank You for establishing my heart unblamable in holiness, causing my ways to be perfect. Faith works by love, so I want my love walk perfected, Lord. You said, "Full-grown (complete, perfect) love turns fear out of doors and expels every trace of terror!" Help me to mature in Your love, in Jesus' name. Amen.

Psalm 18:30,32; Psalm 19:7; Galatians 5:6;

1 Thessalonians 3:12,14; 1 John 4:18 AMP

— CONFESSION —

God's love is the underlying motive
that propels all of my words and actions!

Lord Jesus, when You spoke to the disciples that You had meat to eat that they knew not of, they had no understanding that You were referring to "do the will of him that sent me, and to finish his work." Initially, they thought You were speaking of physical food. The greatest priority in Your life was to do the will of the Father and to *finish His work*. I will follow Your example and put the Kingdom of God first, obey the Father and finish His work – complete the vision – entrusted to me, in Jesus' name. Amen.

John 4:32-34

—————————— CONFESSION ——————————

The greatest thrust of my life is to do the will of the Father and to finish the work to which He has called me!

Heavenly Father, I believe in You and in Your Word. You said that in this way I would be established and prospered. Help me to discern a true prophet from a false one, Lord Jesus, because You said they would exist and they would bring "damnable heresies" into the Body of Christ, by which some of the elect will even be deceived. Quicken me by Your Spirit to be more discerning of the right spirit as well as wrong ones, in Jesus' name. Amen.

2 Chronicles 20:20; Matthew 24:24; 2 Peter 2:1; 1 John 4:1

———————————— CONFESSION ————————————

I am established and prospering because I am anchored into the Word of God, which is my standard of all truth.

Father, I will be wise unto that which is good and simple concerning evil. In Jesus' name I will not recompense evil with evil, but I will overcome evil with good. I will not be a silent bystander when I know something is wrong. Instead, I will be a positive contributor to the dissolution of challenging words and actions. Through the Holy Spirit, I will not only have a word in season, but I will have an effective action in season to pull up the roots of evil and to overcome it with good, in Jesus' name. Amen.

Romans 12:17,21; Romans 16:19

— C O N F E S S I O N —

*I will make it a daily challenge to overcome evil in
a way pleasing to Jesus! I have the shield of faith to quench
all the fiery darts of the wicked. (Rom. 12:21; Eph. 6:16.)*

Father, according to Your counsel through Samuel to Saul, as I stay small in my own eyes or humble before You, You will promote me to the top of the area of assignment in which You place me. You spoke the same principle through James that as I remain humble before You, You will lift me up! I repent of any pride and arrogance, Lord. Help me to be humble before You, whether I am at the top or totally unknown to any man for my work for You, in Jesus' name. Amen.

1 Samuel 15:17; James 4:10

———— CONFESSION ————

Pride and arrogance have no place in me.
I will remain humble before the Lord.

Father God, thank You for the provision of the day in which to work, the night in which to rest. There was an urgency, Lord Jesus, when You said, "I must work the works of him that sent me, while it is day: the night cometh, when no man can work." By the signs of the times, the days are short for the completion of the vision You have called us to carry out. Therefore, I ask the Holy Spirit to orchestrate my daily schedule and energize me so I will complete the tasks that are on God's agenda for me, in Jesus' name. Amen.

John 9:4

———— CONFESSION ————

At the start of each day, I'll synchronize my agenda
with God's, adjusting to His plans for me.

Heavenly Father, You said in Your Word that there is a happy end for the person of peace. My spouse is a peacemaker. He/she exercises great ability and discernment in bringing Your wisdom into our marriage and home, because he/she pursues Your peace, Lord. The atmosphere of our home is filled with harmony instead of strife and discord. It is filled with unity rather than division. It is filled with creativity and excitement, because it is dominated by Your love, Lord Jesus. Hallelujah!

Psalm 37:37; Matthew 18:18-20; 1 Peter 3:11

———————————— CONFESSION ————————————

Because my marriage had God's approval and
He is the central focus of our home, we are living
in an atmosphere of heaven on earth!

Thank You, Father, for the protocol You have given for the family to function at the highest level of love and power. First, You said the husband is the head of the family, just as You are the Head of the Church, Lord Jesus. The wife is to be in subjection to her godly husband, and the husband is to love his wife just as You love the Church. The husband and wife are to be submissive to each other. I will function in divine protocol because I want the highest level of relationship in my marriage and family, in Jesus' name. Amen.

Ephesians 5:21-33

C O N F E S S I O N

My mate and I are heirs together of the grace of life.
Because we live in unity and harmony,
our prayers are not hindered. (1 Peter 3:7.)

Heavenly Father, I am a new person in Jesus Christ. I have crucified my old nature that was set on gaining the world and its approval. I'll not sell my soul for anything the world has to offer. My new nature is committed and diligent in obeying Your call, Father, and in undoing the works of the devil in every way possible each day! I will receive Your reward of approval, Father, in Jesus' name. Amen.

Matthew 16:26-28

CONFESSION

My very breath is from the Father and
for the advancement of His Kingdom in the earth!

Thank You, Father, for making me plenteous in every work of my hand, in the fruit of my body, my work and my land. You are concerned for my welfare, and You actually rejoice over me! Thank You for believing in me. Thank You for opening unto me Your good treasure and for blessing all the work of my hands. In Jesus' name, the blessings of heaven are loosed upon me so I can be a giver into the work of missions – taking the Good News of You, Lord Jesus, to the ends of the earth and meeting the practical needs of starving, poverty-stricken people. I love You, Lord!

Deuteronomy 28:11; Deuteronomy 30:9

———————————— C O N F E S S I O N ————————————

God has blessed me abundantly so that I might be a blessing to others. I'm looking for needs so I can meet them!

Father, thank You for giving Your angels charge to watch over me, to lead me in the way You have prepared for me, to go before me and to keep me in all my ways. You said if I will not provoke the angels You have assigned to me, you will be an enemy to my enemies and an adversary to my adversaries. Thank You, Father, in Jesus' name, for Your provision of angels and for Your protection through them. Amen.

Exodus 23:20-24; Psalm 91:11

——————— CONFESSION ———————

God's angels are working behind the scenes to warn,
protect and deliver me.

Father God, thank You for sending Your Son to give me life, love, protection and adventure beyond anything the world has to offer. Perhaps the keynote statement in all of Your Word that exhibits the trust You desire me to have in Jesus is when His mother spoke to the servants at the wedding at Cana of Galilee, *"Whatever He says to you, do it."* She respected Jesus' authority in the Spirit. She acknowledged His call. Father God, as spiritual leaders in any capacity, help each of us as members of Christ's Body, to respect, strengthen, encourage and receive from Your gifts in one another, without competition, in Jesus' name. Amen.

John 2:5 AMP

———————————— CONFESSION ————————————

*Whatever the Lord tells me to do by His Spirit
or in His Word, I will do it!*

Father God, I want my heart to be perfect in Your eyes, and I want to walk in full obedience to Your Word. Therein lies the keys to success for my life. You said David was a man after Your own heart, Lord. Though he committed adultery and later murder, You still said of him that he was a man after Your own heart! That was because of the genuine repentance and turning from sin that took place in David's life. I accept Your love, grace and mercy today, Lord. I will begin to see myself as You see me: a man or woman after Your own heart, forgiven and fully accepted by You! Hallelujah!

1 Kings 8:61; Acts 13:22

CONFESSION

I am a man (or woman) after God's own heart!

Lord Jesus, You are the baptizer in the Holy Spirit. Every born-again believer has the Holy Spirit residing within him/her, but You have indicated that there is a separate baptism that looses the Holy Spirit upon our lives. It is an empowering from on High that equips us to be bold in witnessing of You. I need this empowering, Lord Jesus. Remove the timidity of witnessing from me, and fill me with Your love, courage and boldness, Lord. In Jesus' name, I will do my part to reroute people from the path to Hell onto the path that leads to Heaven! Hallelujah!

Mark 1:8; Acts 1:8

———————— CONFESSION ————————

I will share Jesus with someone today!

Father, You said that I will give an accounting to You in the day of judgment for every idle word I speak. Idle, as used in this scripture passage, means "unfruitful or barren, ineffective, that which reduces to inactivity." By my words I will be justified rather than condemned, because I ask You, Holy Spirit, to guard my tongue and convict me of "idle" talk, in Jesus' name. Amen.

Matthew 12:36,37

———————————— CONFESSION ————————————

I am making the God-kind of love (zoe)
the aim of every word I speak!

Father, You prepared David for the defeat of Goliath when no one knew him as he watched over his father's sheep. David experienced Your protection as he first slew a lion and later a bear. He knew his covenant with You, Father, and he functioned in it because of an intimate relationship with You. He used the same principles in defeating Goliath in battle when the other soldiers were afraid. Let it be said of me, Father, that I know You and I know Your delivering power as I am courageous to obey You, in Jesus' name. Amen.

1 Samuel 17:1-50

———— CONFESSION ————

I am courageous and unafraid of the challenges
of the enemy, for God is with me!

Lord Jesus, as a standard for my behavior, You said I am to treat others the way I want them to treat me. I want to be loved, accepted and appreciated. I want the gift You have placed within me to be an encouragement to others. I want to be whole in spirit, soul and body. I want my words to be uplifting, positive words as opposed to cutting, degrading words. I want to reflect You, Lord Jesus, through my lifestyle to others so they will want You! Help me to see these same needs in others and help fill those needs, in the name of Jesus. Amen.

Matthew 7:12; Luke 6:31

————————— CONFESSION —————————

The only competition I have in my life is a competitive spirit to whip the devil at every turn.

Heavenly Father, thank You for showing me the principle of binding and loosing in prayer. You have given me authority and power to bind the works of the devil on the earth and to loose Your works into the earth. I'll loose health for sickness and disease. I'll loose prosperity for lack. Divine direction to the person who is floundering in his/her life. Love for bitterness, hate and ill-will. Help me to use the authority You have invested in me for bringing Heaven into the earth, in Jesus' name. Amen.

Matthew 18:18

─────────── C O N F E S S I O N ───────────

In Jesus Christ, I have been given power
and authority to dismantle all of the power of the enemy.
Nothing the devil plans can harm me. (Luke 10:19.)

 **F**ather God, thank You for the open door You have set before me. The doors You open no man can shut, and the doors You close, no man can open. I accept Your direction for my life, Lord. I will walk through the open doors You place before me and be Your representative wherever You place me. I will keep Your Word, and I will not deny Your name, whether You take me to the offices of kings and presidents, or to the homes of widows and orphans who are in need of help. I will serve people wherever You send me, in Jesus' name. Amen.

1 Corinthians 16:9; James 1:27; Revelation 3:7,8

———————————— C O N F E S S I O N ————————————

I will serve God by serving people wherever He leads me.

Thank You for the good news, Father, that as a new creation in Christ Jesus, I am free of condemnation. It is the works of the flesh of the old nature that bring condemnation because of wrongdoing. But now I'm involved in "right doing"! I walk after the Spirit in Jesus' name, and Jesus' acceptance and approval lead me! Hallelujah!

Romans 8:1

——— C O N F E S S I O N ———

The rewards of the Lord are overtaking me
for allowing myself to be led by His Spirit!

Father, You have ordained me for praise! Praise will still the enemy and the avenger. To "still" the enemy means to literally paralyze his attempts to harm me. As I praise You, Lord Jesus, You will move on my behalf and the enemy will become insignificant to me. You are the central focus of my praise and thanksgiving. Your favor is upon me, because the enemy does not triumph over me, in Jesus' name. Amen.

Psalm 8:2; Psalm 41:11

———————————— CONFESSION ————————————

The Lord in His goodness has anointed me
with the oil of gladness! (Ps. 45:7.)

Father, You promised in Your Word that I would not cast my young nor be barren and that the number of my days You would fulfill. Whether it is to walk out the days until the appointed day of the delivery of a child, to walk out my own life to the fullness of days, or to walk out the birth of a vision You have placed within me, it will *not* be aborted. It will come forth in Jesus' name at Your appointed time in the right place. Hallelujah!

Exodus 23:26

------ C O N F E S S I O N ------

The enemy will not abort any activity or event
that is divinely scheduled for my life!

 Heavenly Father, I lay down my own plans for my life, and I accept Your plans for me. I will serve You and follow You as the Holy Spirit leads me. Because of the empowering of the Holy Spirit, I am not afraid to be a pioneer and go where no one has ever gone, to do what no one has ever done. I am not afraid to assume what the world calls "a gigantic responsibility," because You said whatever I ask in Your name, You will do it, Lord Jesus. If it is "Your assignment for me," You will finance it, and the finances will come as I take each step of obedience to You! Hallelujah!

John 12:26

——————— CONFESSION ———————

Because I serve God with a pure
and full heart, He honors me!

Father, You said in Your Word that though my beginning was small, my latter end would greatly increase! You promised to increase both me and my children more and more. One of Your keys to increase is obedience to Your commands, plans and purposes. Though Job went through many trials brought about by the enemy, his latter end increased until he had twice as much as he initially had. Father, I accept Your plans of increase for me and my seed, in Jesus' name. Amen.

Job 8:7; Psalm 115:14

———————— CONFESSION ————————

*God is increasing me daily in responsibilities
and in blessings so I can be a channel of blessing to others!*

Father, You said that the natural man does not receive the things of Your Spirit. They are foolishness to the flesh nature of man. As a person with a new nature — born again in Christ Jesus — I am able to discern the things of Your Spirit. I have Your mind, Lord Jesus, as I daily renew my mind with Your Word. Hallelujah!

Romans 12:2; 1 Corinthians 2:14-16

———————— CONFESSION ————————

I have the mind of Christ, and the wisdom of God is formed within me. (1 Cor. 2:16.)

Heavenly Father, You said You have "due seasons" for me. I will not become weary in well-doing. Then, in due season, I will reap, because I refuse to faint or become weak in my stand for triumph in You. I will not lose heart, for You  will hasten Your Word to perform it, in Jesus' name. My trust is in You, Father, for You are not a man that you should lie. You will keep every promise to me that I am believing to be fulfilled. Thank You!

Numbers 23:19; Jeremiah 1:12; Galatians 6:9

CONFESSION

God loves me so much that He is a shield for me,
my glory and the lifter of my head! (Ps. 3:3.)

Father, thank You for investing Yourself in me. You have also entrusted to me Heaven's wisdom and prosperity in every realm of life – spiritually, socially, financially, emotionally, physically and mentally. As I am faithful to You, Lord, there is no limit to the promotions You have for me right now in the earth. My faithfulness will also determine my assignment in Heaven. Help me to rule well that which You have entrusted to me, in Jesus' name. Amen.

Matthew 25:21

--- CONFESSION ---

Faithfulness precedes honor.
I am faithful in the tasks God has assigned to me!

Father, by the signs of the times and the fulfillment of prophetic events, the day of Jesus' return is near at hand. You said we are to literally blow a trumpet in Zion (in our churches) and sound the alarm to warn people to turn from  their wicked ways and serve You with a heart of submission, obedience and love. Because Jesus' return is near, I will work even more diligently to do everything You would have me do to further Your Kingdom, Father. Hallelujah!

Joel 2:1,15

———————— CONFESSION ————————

I will stand in the gap for others in prayer
to turn their hearts from hell to Heaven!

Father, thank You for giving me Your principles for effective prayer. Jesus gave one of the foremost principles and that is to pray to You, Father, in His name. He said to ask that I might receive so my joy level will be full! Father, in Jesus' name, I ask that You forgive my nation for sanctioning sin in our land. I pray that our government leaders on the local, state and national level will all bow their knees to You, Lord Jesus, acknowledging that You hold the highest office in our land! In You, Father God, we do trust! Amen.

John 14:13-15; John 16:23,24

———————— C O N F E S S I O N ————————

Righteousness exalts my nation! (Prov. 14:34.)

Heavenly Father, because my spirit is in sync with Your Spirit, You are unveiling to me the mysteries of Your Kingdom. I hear and understand, I see and perceive. Just the opposite is true with people who are led by their flesh. Their  ears are dull of hearing and their eyes are closed to the things of Your Spirit. My ears and eyes are blessed! Thank You, Lord Jesus!

Matthew 13:1-16

————— C O N F E S S I O N —————

*Each day I hear, see and understand more
and more of the mysteries of the Kingdom of Heaven!*

Father, You said You would establish me in holiness if I would keep Your commandments and walk in Your ways. Because I am pursuing Your commandments and I am obedient to them, the people who know me acknowledge that I am called by Your name. They see a difference in my lifestyle because I have allowed myself to be set apart for Your Kingdom. Help me to continue to grow spiritually in You, Lord, following Your example and walking in Your footsteps, in Jesus' name. Amen.

Deuteronomy 28:9,10; 1 Peter 2:21 AMP

— CONFESSION —

*I am walking in the footsteps
Christ has prepared for me.*

Heavenly Father, thank You for filling me with Your wisdom which is found in Your Word! Your wisdom causes me to function at a level of intelligence, far above the most highly educated person in the world. Your wisdom is pure, peaceable, gentle, easy to be entreated, full of mercy and good fruits, without partiality and without hypocrisy. I am in a highly esteemed position, Father, to receive and then walk out the wisdom You give to me! Hallelujah!

James 3:17

———————————— CONFESSION ————————————

God's wisdom is one of His daily benefits to me!

Father, I've been out of balance with some of my words. I submit to You for an alignment of my words with Your Word! You told the Israelites who murmured and rebelled against You, "As ye have spoken in mine ears, so will I do to you." When Solomon asked You for wisdom to lead the Israelites, because his heart motives were pure, You said, "I have done according to thy words." Father, help me to create good with my words, in Jesus' name. Amen.

Numbers 14:28; 1 Kings 3:12

CONFESSION

*The mountains of life which I face
will be removed by faith in my heart
and the words of my mouth. (Mark 11:23,24.)*

Father, thank You for the example You gave us in Paul's life. Before setting sail from Crete, Paul warned those in charge of the ship that they should not sail because he perceived there would be trouble – hurt and much damage to the ship, plus loss of lives. Instead of being angry because they did not accept his wisdom, given to him by the Holy Spirit, Paul prayed. He didn't pout or accept rejection. He prayed! Help me to pray instead of adding to existing problems, Lord Jesus. Because of Paul's prayer, though the ship was destroyed, there was no loss of life. Hallelujah!

Acts 27:1-25

CONFESSION

*I believe God and His Word, that what
He has spoken to me will surely come to pass.*

Jeremiah spoke to the people, "Amend your ways and your doings, and obey the voice of the Lord your God." That's a word for me and for all believers in this hour, Lord. It's time to be serious about lining my life up with Your standard of holiness. Help me to be holy just as You are holy. Help me to be moved by compassion just as You are, Lord Jesus. Let my entire purpose for living revolve around pulling others from the kingdom of darkness into Your Kingdom of light, in Jesus' name. Amen.

Jeremiah 26:13; 1 Peter 1:15,16

———————————— CONFESSION ————————————

Holy, holy, holy is the Lord God Almighty,
who was and is and is to come! (Rev. 4:8.)

Heavenly Father, I am standing in the gap for the healing of my loved ones and friends. In Jesus' name, I bind the spirit of infirmity, and I loose Your healing virtue into them. Thank You, Holy Spirit, for interceding and pleading in our behalf according to God's will. Your plan for my loved ones and friends and for me is that we prosper in every way and that our bodies keep well as our souls keep well and prospers, in Jesus' name. Amen.

Ezekiel 22:30; Matthew 18:18; Romans 8:26,27; 3 John 2 AMP

——————————— C O N F E S S I O N ———————————

Jesus Christ took our weaknesses, infirmities and diseases.
Therefore, we can walk in healing and wholeness. (Matt. 18:17.)

Father, Abigail intercepted the wickedness of Nabal, her husband, to protect Your anointed one, David. Let Your champions arise in this hour to intercept and reroute wickedness to protect and deliver Your children from harm. You said in Your Word, Father, that it is not good to touch Your anointed. The wickedness a person plans will return upon his (or her) own head. Cleanse me so I walk uprightly in all the affairs of life, in Jesus' name. Amen.

1 Samuel 25:23; 1 Chronicles 16:22; Psalm 105:15

—————————— CONFESSION ——————————

I will be a gap-stander, in prayer and in action
as the Holy Spirit leads, to intercept wickedness
that is plotted against God's people.

Heavenly Father, like David, I offer You a psalm of thanksgiving for Your goodness and mercy. I will make known Your deeds among the people and talk of Your wondrous works. I will seek Your face continually. Help me  never to forget the covenant I have with You because of Jesus' sacrifice for me on the cross of Calvary. This covenant, based upon relationship, provides everything I will ever need in this life. In Jesus' name, I will give You the glory that is Yours. I will worship You in the beauty of holiness. Thank You for reigning in my life, Lord! Amen.

1 Chronicles 16:7-36

─────────── CONFESSION ───────────

Great is the Lord, and greatly to be praised. (1 Chron. 16:25.)

Other Books by Word Ministries, Inc.

A Call to Prayer
Prayers That Avail Much — Volume I
Prayers That Avail Much — Volume II
Prayers That Avail Much — Special Edition
Prayers That Avail Much for Mothers
Prayers That Avail Much for Fathers
Prayers That Avail Much for Teens
Prayers That Avail Much for Business Professionals
Prayers That Avail Much — Volume I Spanish Edition
Prayers That Avail Much — Volume 1 Portable Gift Book
The Prayers That Avail Much Daily Calendar

Available from your local bookstore, or by writing:
Harrison House · P.O. Box 35035 · Tulsa, OK 74153